If No Moon

CRAB ORCHARD SERIES IN POETRY

Open Competition Award

If No Moon

MOIRA LINEHAN

Crab Orchard Review

&

Southern Illinois University Press

CARBONDALE

09 08 07 06   4 3 2 1

The Crab Orchard Series in Poetry is a joint publishing venture
of Southern Illinois University Press and *Crab Orchard Review*. This
series has been made possible by the generous support of the Office
of the President of Southern Illinois University and the Office of the
Vice Chancellor for Academic Affairs and Provost at Southern Illinois
University Carbondale.

Crab Orchard Series in Poetry Editor: Jon Tribble
Open Competition Award Judge for 2006: Dorianne Laux

Library of Congress Cataloging-in-Publication Data

Linehan, Moira, date.
  If no moon / Moira Linehan.
    p. cm. — (Crab Orchard series in poetry)
  ISBN-13: 978-0-8093-2761-4 (pbk. : alk. paper)
  ISBN-10: 0-8093-2761-9 (pbk. : alk. paper)
  I. Title.
PS3612.I538I35 2007
811'.6—dc22
                                                  2006027188

Printed on recycled paper. ♻

The paper used in this publication meets the minimum requirements of
American National Standard for Information Sciences—Permanence of
Paper for Printed Library Materials, ANSI Z39.48-1992. ∞

In memory of Daniel Ounjian

To have lived it through and now be free to give

Utterance, body and soul—to wake and know

Every time that it's gone and gone for good, the thing

That nearly broke you—

Is worth it all . . .

—*Seamus Heaney, "To a Dutch Potter in Ireland"*

Contents

Acknowledgments

My thanks to the editors of the following magazines, where poems in this collection first appeared, sometimes in earlier versions:

Alaska Quarterly Review—"Pietà" and "Crows"
America—"Boxers Were What My Father Painted" and "For the Rest of My Life I Would Wear Black"
Crab Orchard Review —"Back"
Green Mountains Review—"Late Letter"
Indiana Review —"Penelope"
The Laurel Review—"The Pilgrim's Way" and "Quarry"
The Merton Seasonal—"On Inishmor"
The Nebraska Review—"Letter to Mario Saavedra-Olavarrieta, Now Brother Daniel, Weston Priory, Weston, Vermont"
Notre Dame Review—"Hunger" and "Refuge"
Poetry—"Eve's Design" and "Vow of Stability"
Poetry East—"What He Did for Me"
Sou'wester—"In Praise Of"
TriQuarterly—"Another Waking" and "Memento Mori"

"Pietà" is also forthcoming in *The Eye of the Beholder: A Poets' Gallery,* edited by Maurya Simon and Elizabeth Faith Aamot.

My appreciation to the Millay Colony for the Arts and the Virginia Center for the Creative Arts for the residencies they granted me.

My abiding gratitude goes to Dorianne Laux and Jon Tribble. I also am indebted to many at *Crab Orchard Review* and Southern Illinois University Press for their careful and caring attention to this collection.

I am especially grateful for the wisdom and generosity of those who read and reread many of these poems in earlier versions: Sarah Getty, Helen Trubek Glenn, Ron Goba, Marian Parry, Martha Silano, and Myrna Stone.

In particular, I thank Mary Pinard. In so many ways, this collection simply would never have come into the world without her.

Finally, more than words can express, my appreciation to my many friends and family members for their belief in me and in my poems as I dedicated myself to putting this manuscript together.

If No Moon

Quarry

Keep in mind, no matter where
this story goes, there's a body
at the bottom of the quarry.
Divers saw it, with a second,
weeks ago. They put up markers
to mark the spot, though what that means

in water, I can only guess.
Then early snows, gale force winds
kept the divers from the water
and the bodies. They've now brought up
the first. Look, I want to remind you
if this story starts to drift

toward the quarry in my mind,
there's still that other body
divers found, then lost when the markers
floated loose. *You don't understand.*
In one hundred seventy feet
of water, said the D.A.

to TV cameras, *you can't see*
your own hand in front of you.
One diver's already had a hard time
coming back up. I don't want to think
what that would mean were I to go
under. No one should ever dive

alone. When we were kids,
I'd follow my brother, climb the rocks
above the waterfall and plunge,
still young enough to be transfixed
by plummeting, by my body
on its own, reversing, rising

before—always before—
I hit bottom. And now, well now's
another story, every night
on the news I can't shut off
in time, Quincy Quarry,
mirror of the one in my mind.

I know better than to go in there,
the markers, the ones there were,
shifted, useless. What I imagine
it might be like to go mad,
have no way to come back. But still
that lure, its inviting end: *Go on.*

Go in, under. All the markers
floated loose. A caller told the cops,
If you look in the quarry . . .
Of course I know my own mind,
though I've tossed so much in there,
it's hard to say what I'd bring up.

Things have been down there this long,
why go looking now? Look,
if the D.A. says it's too risky
to go on in freezing waters,
then what's gone on
could have claimed any diver

anywhere along the line—
perhaps me along the line
of what I've been doing here.
The search is now on hold
while they decide if they should drain
the quarry, all one hundred forty

million gallons, though the cost of that's
beyond the city's means. The elusive
other body won't let the cops stop
altogether. Nor will the man
who waits there every day.
In his mind, the body is his

daughter's. The cops claim it's not.
The father, anyone who's lost
someone, must see with his own eyes.
I just want to see this story
settled, so things can get back
to where they were, though they say

nothing will happen now till after
New Year's. Someone's thrown a wreath
on the water, last thing I saw
last night—that floating marker,
the camera moving back
till it was a speck. Till I lost it.

One

Penelope

Mother's on her knees, fitting a skirt—let's say it's that blue
corduroy with the front patch pockets—to my body
that does not yet have a waist or hips. Next she'll take chalk,
mark the seams, then pull each pin out till the skirt is back

to pieces falling to the floor, my mind elsewhere in the silence,
Mother's mouth full of straight pins when she sews. I never
let her teach me that reversal she would work—the pinning
and unpinning to pin again a seam to finally sew,

her knee against the handle that fed the whirring needle—
though I never meant not to. It's just there was no time,
my need always to be elsewhere, anywhere, but the kitchen
where my mother sewed. Bad enough I had to stand there

for the fitting, for the hemming, for the letting down
of hems when I was growing inches by the month. Or maybe
even then, I sensed the undoing that could happen: more
than panels of a skirt, she could let loose, she could let go

of me. I never spoke with her of this. She's long been gone
as have the gods been gone, and my husband, though not gone
to war or wandering, is not present, my husband close
to death, which is why I need to know what my work does:

Keep him alive? Or me faithful? Perhaps both, what Mother did,
not make-work but what I now must learn in middle age:
there is no other work but starting over, which means
to pin and fit and pin again, let out, take in, take up,

the man I wait for never coming back as I knew him,
my husband, who now has left me to draw the line between
vow and need, my memory fixed on the horizon where last
I saw him, piecework in my hands, these pins in my mouth.

Vow of Stability

1.

The preacher says their vow's meant to remind
the greenest grass is what's underfoot, these monks
who sleep in their robes so that when they wake
for whatever dark hour they are to pray,
place does not matter, their business always
at hand, to work, to pray, one and the same,
these monks trying to love barnyard and desk,
altar and field, the raking, the cleaning,
the singing and fasting, tomorrow, next
week and year, always the same, so that place
is all that matters, threshold blurred between
promise and purpose, Vespers and violets
bunched in a jar, these monks, day in and out,
erasing the line between there and here.

2.

My marriage has come to this: staying put,
my husband failing and I, following him
everywhere: into the shower, washing
his back, out of the shower, drying his back,
back to the bedroom, helping him dress, down
each stair, breakfast, pillows propping him up,
the phone, TV at his fingers till I return
from work at noon, at dinner, feeding him
small meals, small bits of news of his shrinking world,
the Red Sox at least keeping us talking,
night and the reverse, all the undoing,
the undressing and drugging to sleep,
my place, in sickness and in health, sorting
laundry, trash and the bills, locking the doors.

What He Did for Me

During those weeks after he came home from the hospital
      for the last time. During those weeks when he could still
            sit on the couch and I was still trying recipes for soups.
During those weeks when I would call, *Lunch is ready,*
      and he could still walk out into the kitchen. During those weeks
            when his doctor still would not say how long,
so I imagined *Always like this* . . . Even then I could say one noontime,
      I'll bring lunch in there and I could hear in his *Thank you*
            he'd been waiting all those weeks for just that.

If No Moon

Often her dying lover falls asleep
before she can tell him what's on her mind—
that nature, say, might be the way ghosts

or gods cross their path: the blood-red cardinal
outside the bedroom window on the snow-
covered roof below, insistent she pause,

wait him out, though flight's at the edge
of what she and the bird would do.
Or if no cardinal, then the moon at its thinnest,

fingernail of light out of the corner
of her eye that won't let her read. Or if no moon,
then wind, wind which pulls down trees across wires,

wires pulled off the house, no heat
for hours, home the place they must leave.
Maybe she'll never be able to tell him

he was an angel sent to cross her path.
Falling in love with him was so weightless
only a game or a god could have asked

she fall back into snow to ready her body
for wings. Yet when she wakes him for his last pills
of the day, what does she say but *Here, my Love.*

Against Asking

Till then I'd never prayed with
someone all those rosaries
after supper the long
month of May do not count
the five of us kneeling on
and on the hard wood floor
getting harder get through this
one *Hail Mary* get over this
Joyful or Sorrowful Mystery
one more the Glorious
days staying light longer *Holy
Mary* all the other children
were running out of their houses
while I was inside a family
that prayed wanting *now*
and at the hour of our death
out outside don't let anyone
ring the doorbell right now

2.

One after the other the long chain
of them oncologist surgeon young
resident nurse even the priest
asking my husband Do you want
someone to talk to *No No No*
I have her her me I could not breathe
in breathe out out out

3.

He said to me *Don't ask me*
to talk but what did that
mean what did I know
now that he was he was
he don't ask me
how I thought of it but I said
Let's pray to our mothers
didn't he have to talk to someone
didn't he didn't I if I if
I knelt on the floor
I could get closer close to
him in that bed when you pray with
the man who's gotten inside you
there are places you want
to go back to I was terrified of
flying each time we'd take off
I'd ask him to pray
to our mothers hadn't they
hadn't they done this before how
many times they'd given us over
to the care of another never
the same as theirs he was
in my hands now each night
we were children ticketed
and tagged for travel alone
who does not talk to the one
sitting next to them on a plane
me I he could not pray for
long it was a long long wait
for our turn we were fastened in there
there was no getting off or out
I must have known I was
giving him back *I could not*
have given him better care
myself said his doctor

as he sat on our couch how
could he sit by patient
after patient lined up to to
I knew don't ask don't don't

Just Name It

No proof this God of ours was ever
on top of things. Just look in the Bible:
wars, famines, boils—you name it.
He's always playing catch up, caught you,
needing, yes, some out-of-proportion
flood, fire, earthquake to rein us in.
What a way to run a world.
Yet aren't they all like that—
those gods before Christ, after,
Christ Himself? How many walked away
for what He would *not* do.
But that's the deal: staying.
On hold so long you don't know
if you still are. Staying.
In the face of, in spite of—
you name it. Like when he—
your husband—was dying.
No 800-number to call.
No proof, just overtime, months
and months of it, digging deep down
to the self you didn't know
was there but there, yes,
if you stay. And stay. Forget
turn-around time. Forget Christ
lifting a finger. Hell'll freeze
first. This is not about deadlines,
beating other guys to market,
just-in-time or backup systems.
It's what's between the two of you
when you're out of time, beyond it

and you see who you could be,
deep down desire, no proof, just name it,
yes, what you want when you have him,
only him, one more day. Go for that.

Letter to Mario Saavedra-Olavarrieta, Now Brother Daniel, Weston Priory, Weston, Vermont

November 1991

Forgive me this letter, such a strident gash,
I'm sure, across your shrouded hills, but I can't shake
what I heard you vow under rafters, barn sides open,
mountains and mist moving in and out, same weather
now over my pond. I should begin, though, by saying
I'd begun to doubt I'd ever find your place
in time to make Mass, my map missing roads,
tourists jamming the single lane south. As the mist

turned to rain, I was sure I should have stayed put,
as if being lost let me see looking
for the right road, right barn in Vermont—your chapel
for wanderers, church I'd wandered away from—
is such a needle in a haystack, the sacred
so resistant to approaches head on. Perhaps that's how
I missed the entrance, backtracked to more than a chapel,
T-shaped barn, posts stained the color of cold rain

and great blue herons. My pond's on their flight path,
those birds like heavy planes that take so long
to get off the ground you think they won't ever lift.
You must be wondering, *Why is she writing?*
That vow to live the rest of your life in one place,
Mexico never again home, has left me so lost.
The rain never let up. *Such a good sign,* you said.
Where you come from the god of rain's the god of life.

You asked us not to take pictures of your guests—
those women, bright blue shawls shrouding their faces,
the men who zigzagged around them, bird's eye view
of my rambling. Your vow to stay put still turns me
in circles, you—so happy to make that vow.
Yet for the longest time you would not stop hugging
your mother, the two of you locked together,
teetering, as Mass started. Had I known that Mass

would last two and a half hours, I would never
have stayed, but by then unable to leave, unable now
to stop circling back to what I heard you vow,
a mist still obscuring what I know should be there.
Maybe it's the name you received at that Mass—
same name as my husband's—has given me license,
writing this letter letting me see what I can't
shake loose is my husband, a meandering cancer

loose in his body, one mass jammed between nerve
and vein atop his right thigh. I tell you, this spring
no one, not even my husband, knew I tried
to break my vow to stay married, tried to find a way
to wander away. He was so hunched over on our couch,
that blue afghan like a shroud around his shoulders,
I was sure he'd never notice I was gone.
You're thinking, *How could you even have thought*

of leaving just when he needed you most?
But as I circle back to your vow to stay till you die,
I see how the heart works as weight against flight,
how it jammed my lift to leave. Though I tried, I could not
leave the stranger he'd become. He's more familiar now.
Yet, when I lie down beside him, my house feels stripped
away, plaster and siding gone. So much weather—
rain, the onset of winter—moves in and out. My bones

know the future: the day my turning toward him
is so jarring he must have his own bed. I'll close
but not without asking you pray I stay faithful
enough so that when I am alone and dying,
his memory will pierce that final mist drifting
around me. Nothing will obscure what has always
been there, my longing to lie down beside only him,
lifting me, letting me rise to him through rafters.

Two

Another Waking

How do I start over? Love again
the light amidst the shimmering
tree shadows? How, when each waking

is so confounding: What's dream? What's
not? Each waking, whipsawing you
at once here and not, light, no shade,

fugitive shivers, moth wings
dusting the lawn, my arms, and then
another dawn. Again I'm turning

toward your side of the bed, at once
knowing grief the way there's sun, a tree,
and off to one side, shadow,

that quiver of a dance, here, no
there, the tree rooted and I, tangled
in the turning toward you gone

and still here, I in bed more
and more of each day. The space
you hold slips between everything,

everything slips through my hands,
moth wings, opening, closing. Moth
that goes nowhere, nowhere to land.

The Route Grief Takes

Thirty days, at most, it will live. And yet,
how much work went into those wings.
The planning it took for the pattern
for this butterfly alone. The involutions
of one black line for one wing, the other
a perfect copy. Such conspicuous
deadly orange, birds learn to stay away.

❖

Monarchs migrate once: north from the equator
if spring, toward it if fall, the entire route
pre-ordained. Once. No sense learning landmarks
when there's no going back. Yet even in this
linear landscape—*Carry the pollen there*—
how much is left to chance. Such dependence
on papery wings. That intimate rubbing.
Not just any hungry flower's throat.

❖

What was it made you expect grief
would be straight-forward by now?
This is only the first summer
you are without him. Four years it took—
more—for his disease to spin its convolutions,
entangle each of his organs. And you.
Now grief's labyrinth. The way out
never mirrors the way in. It could be
you will never know grief as migratory.
Even birds will leave you alone.

For the Rest of My Life I Would Wear Black,

black sweater, black skirt, black nylons and shoes,
and live among women who mourn, meeting—
front stoop, market or street—even in passing,

exchanging a sign otherwise distilled
to sighs, stooped shoulders, grief, always present
and so long worn like a ring, I would miss

its absence. It's time. I should take mine off,
the first year almost passed and it's time
I face strangers alone. He is dead. But

the year's gone too fast and I can't find
one memory where he's not in that bed,
strangers in our house around the clock, him

sleeping or on edge from not. When was it
we were alone, unnoticed, on our way?
He went on dying while I moved through our house,

a sleep walker, but alert enough to catch
the strangers' stares, a study in slow motion.
My ring removed, the callous on my palm

would dissolve. No longer would my body
bear any sign of his passing. I would have
lost him and all trace of him, what's not said,

or said in a hurry, leaving me longing
to hear, *Never was one woman so cherished.*
But who ever speaks that way? In the North End

women in black huddle against shadowed brick
store fronts where skinless rabbits hang upside down,
those featureless widows, their stories, one

and the same. But strangers know their past
without asking, would know mine were I in black,
this story I'd wear for the rest of my life.

Pietà

Galleria dell'Accademia, Florence

Death's weight everywhere
in the body the mother struggles to hold.
Chest muscles knotted in the failed last
heave of his lungs, his cavernous chest
falling against her, his head falling back,
away. Legs withered. If only she could
slide her arm up under his. Who'd ever believe
those shoulders of hers not enormous enough,
Mother of Christ, to handle him dead? Death

already about its work, severing cords
in her wrists and arms, all the way up the line
into her mind till nothing can be grasped,
least of all, Sweet Jesus, what's been placed
in her hands. Yet she's robbed even of that—
time to hold him—sundown fast approaching,
the body, yet to be washed and wrapped.
A wail, starting to rise, wail she won't
ever let loose, turning her to stone.

Two Hearts

No, not just wind, though it's wind
spangles the unmistakable heart
this moment surfaced on the pond,

perfect heart-shape of sequins
in a slinky black shiver.
Then, a second dazzling

next to that shuddering first.
Two jazzed-up hearts that won't let go
their formation and I'm fixed on the stairs,

looking out. No mistaking the dead—
the one man I loved—reaching back,
down or through. No need to know which.

Not when out of the brilliant blue
he's here. This flash dance hurts
my eyes, the million pinwheels

of light, yes, just water and wind,
but looking for all the world
like he's still holding on.

Memento Mori

Near the end he would not stop
stroking my cheek bones, my jaw.
Bedridden, he would not tire

of outlining my lips. Then again,
as if this time he'd get it right.
Those fingers, so weak but holding on

to what he would take with him.
Never had I held so still
as I held out, the world came down

to this man memorizing
my face. There was a time
the grieving had their dead

photographed. Not so bad, perhaps,
to have somewhere to go—
mantle, drawer, locket—

when I longed for, if I forgot
his face. Not his face, death's
door slammed again in my face.

Marking Time

That's the birthday I can't forget,
you—just a few weeks left
to live. Three times I ask you

to wish me a happy one, you
in bed all the time by then, wooden,
your eyes shut. You will not speak

the rest of the day. Always
I'm walking out of the room.
To work. For the doorbell.

You need your pills. You want
a glass of water. Toast. You don't
want toast. Four years have passed.

An osprey came to our pond
for the first time that fall. He sat
in the elm at the water's edge.

By November we could see him
starkly, hunched on that same branch.
We never saw him arrive,

never saw him leave. He was there
watching. And then, not. Like you,
I let that birthday pass without

saying more. How much was left
unsaid. Enough time passed.
We began to expect that bird.

We kept an eye out for him.
Look, I loved to say, *he's back.*
Or, *Look, he's still there.*

Crows

Whoever said *Straight as a crow flies*
never saw the crows in my back yard

zigzag tree to rock wall, garage roof, shrieking
back to wall, branch, gutter, crosshatching the air

in a fury of streaks. Try reading those lines
for a sense of the world, the heart's weight,

what keeps you up in the air, keeps you going
back to where you've just come from. Force-field

around me, below me, this house my husband
died in and left me years ago now, rooms

I still crisscross, pulled as I am by something
in the earth's depths, or maybe much closer:

his body buried two streets away, or those desires
that surfaced screeching, flying every which way

the months he was dying. Just when I think they're gone,
they're back *en masse* in swoops, shrill as ever.

The Pilgrim's Way

Monastery of Our Lady of Gethsemani, Kentucky

Each fall, that schoolroom lesson on seeking
never finished, the Pilgrims' journey
not done at landfall, there the new bewildering

winter. How many times I find myself lost
south of Louisville, too many route numbers
missing or missed the closer I come to where

I know Merton lived his cloistered life,
writing book after book on the unending way
he'd made his way toward the sacred. Back home

in England, those Pilgrims had fed their faith
on so much defiance it's hard to say
which drove them to seek their passage or what

happened when doubt insinuated itself,
doubt always snaking over the cold rocks
at the back of the heart. I mean Merton

seemed so willing a pilgrim, those farmlands
harboring his cloister—their seasons of clear
and plant, only to clear again—had to have kept

his journey going to the day he died.
The day he died, my husband set me
on a ship no known country will let dock.

The watery part of the voyage over,
the Pilgrims knelt on such wilderness
they had to name it what they knew, a name

to locate them between what was and what
was to come. No name I attach to mourning
moors it. Yet there was never any doubt

I'd lose my way, my husband always the map
reader. How many times I have to stop,
ask for directions before I finally see

the white buildings set against, rising above
the land. Mourn long enough, grief loops back
on itself, its journey, the recurring

crisscrossing of what I remember
just passing. Each morning the monks' chant,
one side of the shadowy chapel,

then the other and back, bells tolling
for the missing. For those present: *Begin now,*
those monks in a constant returning to where

they were just an hour, a year ago,
seeking anew the meaning of this passage
from Scripture. From this world. The monks' quarters

off-limits, I wander old logging trails
surrounding their cloister, each leading me
back to the gate near the chapel, full circle,

back home, the unending opening
the door. The going in, and in once more.

Three

Dread

Even Vikings would not come ashore
in such weather—howling winds
heaving the sea out of its depths,
cavernous waves hurtled headlong

against rock face cliffs. Ireland,
boxed in and pummeled by yet another
storm, but the monks' dread of calm
seas, submerged in the fury, such weather

respite, letting them return to oratories
and manuscripts, work that will survive
a millennium. Same ancient weather
moving out as I arrive late June

for two weeks, the departing storm
trailing a gray winding sheet—dank
fingerings along the back of my neck.
It's been wicked here, says an old woman

hanging her still lifes one by one
on the fence around St. Stephen's Green.
*So wicked you could emigrate
and never come back. Or murder yourself.*

The storm's wintery wake hangs back.
The next wave rolls under, begins to swell.

Refuge

Inhospitable land, inhospitable people.
—Guidebook, Aran Islands

I was going there for its widows
or its history of widows,
concentration of them on that island
where men once fished the North Atlantic
alone, only work there was with the land
stone. Each in his curragh, rowing—
sometimes for days—while the women waited
for them to return. To go back out.
A woman could go mad in that place.

        I was going there
where monoliths to men lost at sea
line roads, the history of widows
cut in stone. In the soul
patterns of dread—men present, then not—
passed mother to child. These women
who knit in doorways. At row's end,
turning the piece to purl. Stitches
named for things of land: seed, moss,
blackberry. Sweaters taking shape.

        I went there
a widow, the women still knitting
though now for tourists, same family
patterns, no two alike. (How else
know the body washed up?) These women
holding needles the way their mothers—
and their mothers before them—did,
giving shape to their prayers, each row
a rosary, naming the body.

                              I stayed
a week though I could not speak
the language. In earlier times
those caught using Gaelic
had the tips of their tongues cut off.
That terror—what could be lost if
the heart spoke—can be passed down,
silence a people, make a stone
(widow that I am) feel at home.

Still Missing

Naturally, I saw my dad on Inishmor:
fair, fine-boned old man above the harbor,
sweaters layered on, staring out to sea.
Dead fifteen years, yet showing up now
and then as the dad I knew near the end:

turned toward the hereafter, believing
what had always eluded him was close at hand.
Never as the dad who'd held me, run along side
me on my first bike, then let go so I would
get the hang of balance. Never as the one

who'd put his arms around mine, held the bat
with me till I could connect on my own.
Who'd taught me to read clouds for flying rabbits,
witches' cauldrons, whales. Who'd written my name
on the backs of turtles we turned back to the woods,

on the inside covers of books, wet sand
at Lighthouse Beach. But showing up last week
outside the post office, an old man by himself,
his head in his hands? The dad I knew
would never have displayed so much emotion

on a public bench, though that's whom I see.
An old man already dressed for winter,
stopping me, making me wonder if that's not
heaven's surprise for him: something still
missing—now his lost and only daughter.

Boxers Were What My Father Painted,

in his body knew their dance, that measure
of approach and backing off they weave, gloved hands
cupped around their bobbing faces till the arm
goes straight for the slam. One Christmas

he bought my brothers boxing gloves. I got to tie
the long white laces and watch, my father
telling one to throw some kind of hook,
the other to hold his arm just a little

higher while he sketched heavy men in trunks
inside a ring. My mother could not stand
to hear us in the cellar so we moved
to the field behind our house because my father

could not stop painting boxers, how he saw them
in his sons, my brothers, all arms and gloves
intertwined, painting boxers till the year he died
though he never sold one painting, other wives

and mothers likely saying no to hanging fighters
over fireplaces. Years later, dividing up
the only home we'd ever known—boxing gloves
tossed in with silverware and sideboards—

my father brought his children back together,
my brother Joe having backed way off, his way
of being son and brother, though he was working out
at the Y, jumping rope, he said, and boxing.

Ireland

For years the night conductor on the Metro North
out of New Haven, my brother Joe's got stories
that keep us at the table. Holidays. After wakes.
He tells each like it's the one good one he has.
The guy who murdered his mother, cut her up

and stuffed the pieces into trash bags, then hopped
a train—Joe's train—to pick a fight, alibi
for his whereabouts when the cops came knocking.
Well, Joe's the one he picked to punch, so *Next stop
Stamford,* Joe throws him off. But first he must report him

to the train police, then to Stamford's. Now you should know
my brother's had his share of run-ins with the cops,
when he was younger, spent time in jail sleeping off
nights of drinking, though that's a story for another time.
This night the cops are asking a guy who has just

cut his mother up into a hundred pieces, *How'd he,*
as they point to Joe, *treat you?* As if they know
Joe's record. But this guy wants to be the one
who has a record, so he makes sure the cops write down
what he did. And when. And there's Joe, at it again,

holding us in suspense while he takes his own sweet time
getting to the end. How many times he's sucked me in,
telling me yet another story, this time
my husband's wake finally over, holding my in-laws
in a circle close to him, me on the outside,

listening in, in spite of myself. Joe, who never once
stepped inside my house the whole time my husband took
to die, now at the part where the cops've found the body—
well, you know what I mean—and they've come knocking
at Joe's door, *to ask me,* Joe says, *what he looked like*

when he first got on the train. I know what they want
to hear, so I tell 'em, Joe says, he swears he tells them,
"He looked like a guy who could have just murdered
his own mother." And they write it down, Joe says.
They write it down, though Joe, being the storyteller,

I often wonder what's real and what's his doing.
But I never wonder about his way with words,
his art for grabbing someone—strangers, even me.
He did it again just last week on the phone,
this time the story of an old man in a wheelchair

at the Branford Hospice. *I was there on Saturday,*
he's saying, *to hang my show.* Did I tell you
my brother paints? Paints everyday. Geraniums
in a window box across the street. Hollyhocks
up close. A porch Hopper might have done.

But I was telling you about the hospice.
Do you know what a hospice is? Joe asks,
though he does not wait for me to answer,
going on about his paintings—twenty-five of them—
lined up in the hallway. *I'd gone back to the lounge*

to take a break when I see a wheel. Then a shoe
and pants leg. Then this old guy in a wheelchair
coming round the corner. He's crooking his finger
for me to follow him, so I do, to my painting
of the thatched roof cottage. You know the one I mean?

He's pointing and he's whispering, he's whispering
in the lowest voice I've ever heard till I get,
I finally get he's saying "Ireland." Joe stops a moment,
then goes on. *Later the Director comes to find me*
to tell me I've worked a kind of miracle. He'd been there

for weeks and not said one word. Not to anyone.
After he'd talked to me, he'd gone to find her . . .
which is where Joe ends this story about a place
he's never seen but painted from a photograph.
Before he hangs up, Joe asks again if I know
what a hospice is, as he whispers one more time, *Ireland.*

On Inishmor

In the village of Kilronan
on Inishmor. In the church
in the village of Kilronan
on the island of Inishmor,
far west as you can get
in the Atlantic and still
be in Ireland, the nave's ceiling's
the open rib work of a curragh
overturned on shore, capsized
at sea. Where the sea's the only work,
a boat's the one sure thing
that can be shaped. And dread.
I know my mother's. Her first child,
first daughter, never came home
from the hospital. I came
the next year. Perhaps, too soon.
Perhaps, not soon enough. *Who*
will be next? Two more
after me would live. Two more
would not. Today, unrelenting gales
have driven me mad for refuge
into this church, the clouds—
unyielding stone like the land.
Here, where there's no frost,
nothing's needed to hold stone
on top of stone, become walls,
turning small plots of cleared land
smaller parcels, three or four
thousand miles of these walls,
maze where I get trapped
more than once when I climb
toward the cliffs. There, of all places,

no walls line the edge.
The terror of losing hold
holds me back. I have
lost hold, the one man I loved,
taken, leaving me without
walls. The winds won't let up.
Here, where men built boats
that might not bring others back,
they built a church's vaulted ceiling
the exposed bowed bones of one
overturned, capsized, as if they believed
praying were like righting a curragh,
each morning nothing else to do
but cast off into the deadly cold keep
of the North Atlantic.

Hunger

> ... the long nights he spends in his curragh bring
> him some of the emotions that are thought peculiar
> to men who have lived with the arts.
> —J. M. Synge, *The Aran Islands*

Alone in his boat,
lines listless. Ancient mended nets,
only so much they can take in, hold.
Night's ribcage pressing. Swells, sheer as the Cliffs
of Moher. At any moment he could go under
and no one would know. Not for days. Weeks, maybe.
No use going back, though, when the land's stone.

Ropes lashed round his waist,
he's lowered over the exposed edge
of a cliff. He'll take his place on a ledge
slippery with droppings, among brooding seabirds,
to rob their nests. All this happens by night.
Weather can strand him. Bringing him back up
is slow going. Even the young ones
know of men squalls smashed against the rocks.

Going Back

Zucchini thick as baseball bats, tomatoes,
yellow squash, of course eggplants—nothing
exacting about ratatouille—all
waxy vegetables. And onions. Bacon
very well cooked and crumbled, crushed garlic.
Untold spices and herbs—oregano, basil,
then parsley, black pepper, dash of red and this

sudden sadness at my stove, my mother un-
reachable across the span of forty years,
quince-colored light from the afternoon's late sun,
preserves—yes quince, but also peach, plum, blueberry
on the long basement shelves at Delsole Road.
Now it's a Mason jar of applesauce

my mother's opening—chunks of apples,
loads of cinnamon swirled in. Memory, so
kaleidoscopic. Only the slightest turn,
just like that, she's seated at her easel
in the basement, a still life in progress—
heavy grapefruit on a linen napkin,

green Mateus bottle, glass stopper. Then she just
fades as now from my kitchen, always fading
exactly when I most need her. Like the day she
died. Sure, I'd left home, but not really. I, her first
child to live. She could never hold me enough.
Back, just once let me be back in her clutch, her
assurance I can go anywhere, she'll still be there.

Legend

Mostly legendary—what's known of him,
though there is a gospel that bears his name
and this basilica, gold Byzantine puzzle
my brother Mark's named after. In those days
a saint's name was required for baptism

so my mother met the letter of the law,
but pagan—was it not?—to choose a place
as namesake, even if it was consecrated.
This, now the second time I've traveled here,
thinking this time I'd find it, my mother's love

for this place. Loot is what it is:
columns, capitals, candelabra, chalices
and, says the legend, the saint's body—all
stolen by merchants from worlds to the East.
This church, built to house his sarcophagus

(if it was his), brought here from Alexandria.
Tradition says he founded the Church there,
worked miracles believed to be magic,
so he was dragged through the streets till he died.
Martyred. What's ever what it seems? This—

once a pantheon and private chapel
for doges, its marble floors now undulating
like streams. What's there to love here? No, one day
and thirty-four years from the day she died,
my mother's basilica is as blank

as the nameless saints surrounding its cupola.
Their black staring eyes yield nothing of what
they know. Shouldn't such excess—sixteen
sanctuary lamps burning at one side altar—
have been the last place she loved, my mother

who wore only a trace of lipstick and powder,
two rings for jewelry? Turned round and round
that rainy afternoon last November
by the city's twisted paths, I'd just wanted
to find my hotel. There was nothing there

for my taking. Well, possibly a patron,
its saint of a writer, though last night I read
he wrote his gospel in Rome where some claim
it was dictated to him by St. Peter.
What's ever what it seems? What's this poem

but a mosaic of stories and spoils
when it was a legend I'd been after,
key to let me locate somewhere, anywhere
on that garish, slippery map of Venice
the stranger, once—long ago—my mother.

Four

The New Part

If I'd read her acknowledgments before
I bought it—last minute purchase in case
of just such a moment (waiting for water
to recede, my hotel's first floor, all first floors
in Venice flooded to the knees that morning)—

I would not have been stuck. Right away
her thanks to a friend for lessons on grief,
for patience as she asked and re-asked her questions,
put me on guard. Granted, it's her province
to dream plot and character, imagine

a widow, her story. But not mine.
I want her to know, I want you to know
my story's not there for anyone's taking.
Of course, I read it. I told you I was stuck
at high tide that morning of the full moon,

morning after. Once the tide turned, the water
drained in an hour and I was out again,
following the twisting canals. Alone.
It took me no time at all to get lost
in the novel, after only a few pages

the heroine, widowed. Then my story
took over. For weeks afterwards I, she,
did not move from our beds. After that, we went
our separate ways, her author lifting her
up and out, into the arms of another

after only a year, while in my story—
this is the part she, you, I, could never
have imagined: six years later, Venice
like home, where ever so gradually
I continue to sink. Six years and the floods

of longing still wash over me as if
I, too, were this gilded watery city,
though here's the *new* part: lately the waters
recede, sometimes for weeks, all on their own,
or maybe it's the moon's doing. No need

to describe what was left behind. Each evening
by the time I returned, even the walkway
had been washed clean. Lamplight flooded it all—
crumbling facades, cambered bridges, murky
canal. Yes, the romance reached even me.

Back

This, after all, is how I came back,
back into place in this world, all suckle and juice—
plum, tomato, chilled wine, even plain water
dribbling down my chin. How long was I gone
in my grief? Almost too long, but back now
in time. Find me. Follow me. I've a tale
of passage through. This roadside barrier—
barbed wire fence, brambles and briars—
mirror of where I long was: tangled
in vines twisting and twisted around vast trunks,
climbing up from the soil, down from branches;
vines thick as clothesline, thin as fiber.
I'm here to report no one comes back
except by desire, that sinuous pleasure
snaking along each limb, leading you forward
and back as you reach for ripe peach, dark grapes.

Understory

All the lore about the season, spread out
on the forest floor, spring on the verge
of arriving above in the old oaks
and maples shoehorned in among the pines,
but here below, crawling up and out
from layers of pine needle rust and leaf-rot:
ferns, fiddleheads, mayflowers, whatever
creeps—all grasping light, as much as they can
before the canopy fills in. This under-
story where spring's exploding at the core
of low-lying plants, energy from the sun's
red and blue bands, only the radiant ends
of the spectrum, my field guide says, being
absorbed, never the middle rays, that is,
never the green. But how even begin
to see green that way—this trailing array,
liquid gushing, lush with longing, oh so much
green upon green as merely reflection
of what's not taken in, what's always missing?

Eve's Design

Then there's the Yemeni legend
of Eve in the Garden knitting
a pattern on the serpent's back,
the snake unfinished like the rest
of creation, the first woman
thinking to add design, a sheath
of interlocking diamonds and stripes
along that sensuous *S*,
knitting giving her time to learn
what's infinitely possible
with a few stitches, twisting cables,
hers a plan to mirror the divine
inner layer that can't be shed
no matter what it rubs up against.

All Over Again

Were I to be killed tonight in a crash
as I head back up the expressway, or choke
on Chinese noodles I re-heat for supper,
or simply never wake up tomorrow—

I confess the way I see you is bounding
down a heavenly hallway, dressed in white
and tanned as ever, tennis balls tucked away
in each hip pocket, yelling, *What took you*

so long? I can't find my hat! Where's my hat?
And without a second thought, I fall right in
and find your hat, your hand already tight
on my arm, telling me about the sunsets,

the choir, the crossword puzzles you've saved—
French phrases, the names of medieval saints
only I can fill in. *Come watch me whip*
this guy, you say, never thinking for a moment

I might first want to find my mother. I have to
admit, my Love, nothing has changed. You're close
to skipping with delight to have me back
and, of course, I fall all over again

(I can't help it) for your boundless embrace
of whatever place you're in, how you want me,
only me, next to you. All this time without
you, though, has made me see you'll never—

even in heaven—turn and ask, *How were those years
for you?* Yet back with you, what would they matter?
At last I'd be letting them go. See, Love,
already contrails are foaming in their wake.

Back into Place

Away all April, I can't say how long
she sat there. But for fourteen days in May,
the swan did not move, her massive white mound
nesting on the opposite shore, mornings

when I got up, throughout the day each time
I checked. The male stayed close, circling, feeding
off plants below the pond's surface. Cygnets
take to the water right away, her two—

day one—dingy puffs swimming behind her
as she hugged the far shore. By the time they reached
my side of the pond, their small bodies had form,
necks already regal and long. Water,

you could say, was their element. Not so the air.
At least, not yet. But I'm getting ahead
of my story. Had I known the young would not fly
till late September, I could have traveled with more

ease those times I was away this summer—
not far, not long—yet not wanting to miss
that first lift off this pond, the young still gray-brown
but close to full grown by mid-summer.

The mother never left their sides. The father
patrolled in front, keeping the geese away.
So it's not clear how one came not to be here
one August day. *A snapping turtle,* guessed my neighbor

to close that part of the story. Then for weeks
little else changed. The cygnet's grayish tone paled.
It never turned white. The days grew shorter.
Each day it did not fly made it that much

harder to go anywhere, though in the end,
I was here for its first moment in air—
not far, not long, more a wavering just inches
above the pond, but oh so clearly out

of the water. Still, I would know that
only after the fact, this bird—right away,
dropping back to the only place I had known
it to have, rearing up and up, wings spread

as it back-pedaled, then settled down,
folding, refolding wing over wing,
craning its neck around, nipping the wide
expanse on its back back, back into place.

Ars Poetica

Undoing all of yesterday's work—
never do I just knit straight through—ripping
row upon endless row back to my error,
a knit instead of purled stitch, now glaring
violation in this lengthening afghan.
In turn, though, even ripping loosens its own
soothing rhythm: bring one stitch at a time
here to the end of the needle, with the other
(easy now) reach in, lift off the loop as you
draw out the strand of yarn. Metronome set,

beating steady slow measures, working in
reverse till I get back to where I want to be ...
(Is any work ever straightforward?
Dancing? Just moving around in circles.
Easing into the ocean each June? Toes in,

out; feet in, out; it can take hours. Penelope's
faithfulness? So much unweaving. Yeats's

quarrel with himself? Murmuring on and on
until he found the rhythm he wanted.
I destroy much of what I do, he said, *continually.*
Entire lines, stanzas, probably whole poems dropped) ...
till I get back to where I can turn it around,
now begin (again) the measured rowing forward,
eventually the pattern re-emerging as I
settle back here before my picture window,
shifting right needle to left this comforter.

In Praise Of

ambiguity. Gradual arrivals.
Black fading back from black. Filigreed branches
coming clear, but just barely, low hill to the east,
dawn—still a dark, draped wrap (or night that won't leave).
Elm there, though—seen or not—at the pond's edge.

Frost on the window, film. Fog coming in. Praise, too, for
gloom and gloaming, gray anything that takes away
heaven, even the here-and-now pond. And praise for
impossible proofs, improbable tales: your
just-dead beloved, dream door ajar, slipping back—

kaddish constantly on your lips, keeping him close and
like a line lengthening out to infinity.
Mergansers may be the best mirror of the black and white
not here/here. Nothing more distinctive than those heads,
one minute swimming along, then under—one, two. Too long.

Possible: this time they won't pop back up. Praise, then, every
quiver of a question that death or just a late rising moon
raises. Or . . . Or . . . Endless rub of oars in their locks.
Shadows and shivers, like spurts of chimney swifts sweeping
through, down, over what you hold dear. So praise what trips

up, what upends. Whatever leaves you unable—
vertigo, gravity, November rains. All the un-
winding winters, ice you can't skate on yet. Still. The dangling
X's and O's that never add up. X'd out chances.
Yo-yoing luck, back out of reach. In the end, praise
zen roads to nowhere. Gabriels all from another realm.

Late Letter

My Love, I've never told you about the last time
I saw her—the poet who'd taught me not to let go
of an image. It was too late in the game (as some
might say), so I never asked that you forgive me

for letting her in. She'd been showing up—one day,
then another, often enough for me to think
she'd be here afterwards to help me go back, line
by line, into your story and out to the other

side. I don't want to begin by eulogizing her,
though she was killed in a crash within weeks
of your dying. Others have already done that—
drawn achingly eloquent scenes of her cities,

evoking their signature siren roils. Evoking hers.
The story I want to tell you starts with black glass beads
I've fingered now for years. I'd heard too many tales
of her addictions not to hide your drugs when she

began ringing our doorbell. You'd have done the same.
Look back, she taught me. *See what's already there.*
Those tiny beads. Her necklace, she'd said, had come unstrung
while she was in the bathroom. She'd come out, loose beads

in hand, asking, *Can you believe it just did that?*
At the time, I did. I still long to. But days afterwards,
on my knees, washing the floor in there, I found five
black beads at the back of the bathroom closet. Then,

days after you died, she phoned from a conference.
She'd befriended a lost soul who'd turned around
and stolen her drugs, prescriptions for on-going pain.
She must really have needed them, she told me.

My teacher's must not have been enough, for there she was,
there was my teacher asking what I'd done with yours.
Black glass beads scattered on the floor of the closet.
Morphine patches I'd hidden, I'd already turned back

to Hospice before she . . . My teacher, the poet—
so often strung out. Yet how often she returned
to her desk, there to string the fractured and shattered
remains of her world into long, looping lines.

For the length of one poem, all her gorgeous,
dangerous links would hold, a necklace of glass
beads. Forgive me, my Love. That's why I let her in.
How else was I ever going to turn ashes

into even one obsidian word for you?

Notes

The two situations described in "Hunger" are largely "found" poems from Synge's *The Aran Islands*.

The field guide referred to in "Understory" is Chet Raymo's *The Path: A One-Mile Walk through the Universe* (New York: Walker and Company, 2003). It is Raymo's explanations there of understory and photosynthesis that I used in this poem.

Other Books in the Crab Orchard Series in Poetry

Muse
Susan Aizenberg

Lizzie Borden in Love
Julianna Baggott

This Country of Mothers
Julianna Baggott

White Summer
Joelle Biele

In Search of the Great Dead
Richard Cecil

Twenty First Century Blues
Richard Cecil

Circle
Victoria Chang

Consolation Miracle
Chad Davidson

Names above Houses
Oliver de la Paz

The Star-Spangled Banner
Denise Duhamel

Beautiful Trouble
Amy Fleury

Pelican Tracks
Elton Glaser

Winter Amnesties
Elton Glaser

Always Danger
David Hernandez

Red Clay Suite
Honorée Fanonne Jeffers

Fabulae
Joy Katz

Train to Agra
Vandana Khanna

For Dust Thou Art
Timothy Liu

Strange Valentine
A. Loudermilk

Dark Alphabet
Jennifer Maier

American Flamingo
Greg Pape

Crossroads and Unholy Water
Marilene Phipps

Birthmark
Jon Pineda

Year of the Snake
Lee Ann Roripaugh

Misery Prefigured
J. Allyn Rosser

Roam
Susan B. A. Somers-Willett

Becoming Ebony
Patricia Jabbeh Wesley